In the image

Portraits of
Mediaeval Women

Alwyn Marriage

Indigo Dreams Publishing

First Edition: In the image: Portraits of Mediaeval Women
First published in Great Britain in 2017 by:
Indigo Dreams Publishing Ltd
24 Forest Houses
Halwill
Beaworthy
EX21 5UU
www.indigodreams.co.uk

ISBN 978-1-910834-41-1

British Library Cataloguing in Publication Data. A CIP record for this book can be obtained from the British Library.

Designed and typeset in Palatino Linotype by Indigo Dreams.
Cover design by Ronnie Goodyer at Indigo Dreams
Printed and bound in Great Britain by: 4edge Ltd
www.4edge.co.uk

Papers used by Indigo Dreams are recyclable products made from wood grown in sustainable forests following the guidance of the Forest Stewardship Council.

Acknowledgements

Chiara and *Godgifu* were first published by the 'Women's Literary Culture and the Medieval Canon' website, February and October 2016.

The first live performance of *Chiara* was at Ways with Words, July 2016.

Hildegard: doctor of the Church was first published in 'Hildegard, visions & inspiration', edited by Gabriel Griffin, Wyvern Works 2014.

Hildegard was subsequently displayed in Winchester Cathedral when I was Poet in Residence for the 10 days Arts Festival there in 2015.

With thanks to Professor Diane Watt of the University of Surrey for encouraging me to put this collection together.

Also by Alwyn Marriage:

Rapeseed, Stairwell, 2017
Notes from a Camper Van, Bellhouse Books, 2014
festo: celebrating winter and Christmas, Oversteps Books, 2012
Touching Earth, Oversteps Books, 2007
Bible Best (ed), Feed the Minds, 1998
The People of God: A Royal Priesthood, Darton, Longman & Todd, 1995
New Christian Poetry (ed), Collins, 1990
Life-Giving Spirit: Responding to the Feminine in God, SPCK, 1989
Beautiful Man, Outposts Publications, 1977.

CONTENTS

Chiara
Clare of Assisi: 1194-1253

Boy Beautiful;
Oh, my boy beautiful.
My study in brown
but no, not mine,
not then, and certainly
not now.

Young as eternity,
old as the crooked wisdom
of the stars
shining through
the darkness and infinity
of our midnight sky

brown eyes that peered
deep into my eyes and pierced
my soul – the soul
I then believed I had
but now am not so sure –
discovering the truth of me
which even then a part of me
knew to be untrue
because you never quite
uncovered the nature of
the fierce devotion
that I offered you.

Brown hair, so soft,
that flopped
across your forehead.
Given half a chance,
how gently it would tickle
a girl's bare stomach, trace
the line from navel down

to where a coarser fuzz
keeps guard,
protects her inner sanctum
like the line
along which you once led me
to the love of God.
Yes, yes, I'll worship Him
of course, sing praises,
celebrate the love divine,
self-giving passion
and the unity of all that is.

~

I knew it wasn't
only me; he touched
the heart of everyone
he met: the shop keeper,
his parish priest, the general
when he went to be a soldier,
the dog that followed
everywhere he went,
the bird that perched
on his left shoulder,
the mouse behind the wainscot
and squirrel in the tree,
chickens and geese, pigs, sheep
and cows, all followed
everywhere he went
and watched him lovingly.

When he was tired and thirsty
the sterile cow let down her milk
the half-lame donkey bore his burden
willingly.
Even before I heard him preach,
he deepened my devotion

simply through the child
of God he was.
I loved God for him
while he loved me
for God.

That thought
did not occur to me
then – I'm sure it didn't;
I'm just looking back
and trying to make sense
of all that love,
look for clues
that might suggest
when and how I lost it
to a higher one.

He caught religion
like the chickenpox;
I watched it spread
through all his being,
and willingly breathed his germs,
greedy to share his joy and suffering.
And when I caught this same
religious passion from him,
I picked it up and ran
to prove that I could love his God
as much as any boy or man.

~

God our Father
all-seeing and all-knowing,
whose never-sleeping eye
searches out our secrets:
you knew the size and shape
of my devotion, even though

I did not, do not, maybe
never will. Cleanse me from
iniquity, or reassure me
that it was not sin.

Jesus my Saviour,
who bled for me,
felt pain and passion
in your living dying body
as you offered love,
both human and divine.
Is it possible to sanctify
this love of mine?

Holy Spirit of God,
whispering between the green
leaves, hinting at what's possible
if not desirable, giggling when
we get the message wrong.
Breathe on me
until your holy inspiration
becomes my only guide.

Holy Mother of God,
following in faith
the dictates of the love
that moves the sun
and other stars.
If, as I suspect,
in the deepest corner
of your heart you do not
condemn me, pray for me now,
and at the hour of my death.

As you see, I could do it all,
and meant it too, in the innocence
and energy of youth.

Daily my devotion grew,
my fasting, hours of prayer
and acts of charity.

~

In his imagination he could see
a world of peace and love;
I followed faithfully,
not realising that in the paradise
he dreamed and planned
there'd be no room for me.

I should have known
when he became a soldier,
talked of triumph,
followed the blaring trumpets
into battle
in search of glory.

What news of war, Beloved?
Blood flowed, he said.
There were so many dead.
One day I saw two sparrows
and a soldier with a catapult ...
Here I had to lean my ear
close to his lips to catch the voice
that choked as he continued,
threatening to fade away.

Day by day I watched the whispering
poplar trees, the swaying of the long
sad tresses of the weeping willows,
the oak that turned its back
on acts of war and stood
faithful and unvanquished
in the field of blood.

One day a horse lay screaming,
shuddering with pain that he
had neither caused nor chosen,
for animals do not inflict
unnecessary suffering
on each other. For love of life,
of God, of the beauty of the world
I had to end his pain, dispatch
him to a better place.
When I close my eyes
I still see visions of that world
which I knew was not what
it was meant to be.

~

And so the unsuitable soldier boy
was returned to me.
But he was changed, could not
accept the life his parents planned
for him, was driven to distraction
by his fine brocade and silk.
When he stripped
to return this finery
to his irate father,
I hid and watched,
held my breath to see
how far he'd go. But no,
there was one garment
left to cover what I'd never
seen. The rest was left
to my imagination.

Later, as he gazed into my eyes
his fingers threaded through my hair
and mine through his.
My hair, so thick and soft,

fell in waves and tresses
to catch an unwary boy.
He stroked it lovingly;
how could he then bear
to let it fall
until my head was bare,
could be covered for
its modesty
only with a wimple?

And how could he, or anyone
love me now I'd lost
my crowning golden
glory? not lost
but shorn in such a futile
but dramatic act
of sacrifice?

He stroked my naked head
so tenderly, sending shivers
down my spine,
prickles of uneasy pleasure
in a place I can't define.
Poor Clare he murmured,
and again, *Poor Clare*,
before he turned and walked away.

I stayed there, watched
the light fade on my hopes
until I felt the chill of night
entering my bones.

~

They say you only miss
the carnal act when you have
known it. My body never has

been swept into that song,
and yet I've relished it
in secret in my heart.
I yearn for it,
was born for it,
dread that I will one day
burn for it,
that when my days have finished
I will feel the fires of hell for it.

That I should wish to be forgiven
for loving him in whom I saw
the light of Christ,
Oh Lord have mercy
Christ have mercy
Lord have mercy
on me.

He was so free and happy,
a feral creature, never to be tamed.
For a while I was content to be
his bird in hand, but learnt too late
the falcon never can enjoy
the freedom of the eagle.

No monastery walls could hold
his spirit, no fabric
rough enough to irritate
his skin;
so he imagined that I too
was bigger than the stones
that bound me, would never miss
the soft and silky clothes I wore
in my father's house.

I am not, in truth, a prisoner:
it was my choice, or so I thought.

What can I offer now?
What gift can I bestow
on the only one I ever loved?

Each chapter in the manuscript
we treasure begins with an initial
whose intricate beauty leads us on
to meditate on all that follows.

And so I live my life
of purity and solitude
in such a way that, though
he cannot see me, he will know
I do it all for him, that others
will be drawn towards his God
because of me.

~

The more I now protest
that I'm not worthy
the more they praise
my sweet humility
and take me for a saint.
Only my confessor knows.
He sometimes scolds
a little, but I think
he understands
and reassures me that the veil
between the love of God
and what I feel for this sweet
child of God is thinner than
the vellum in the sacred Gospel
that I kiss each day.

And then I wonder how this old
and holy man can feel so keenly

the maidenly confusion of my heart.
Do others suffer love as I have done
and do?

Sometimes he gives me for a gentle
penance the recitation of a prayer
that seems to me more like a poem
in which I offer all the pain
and longed-for pleasure
to a God who pours on us
the gift and curse of love.

~

When the ripe corn of my young love
has shrivelled, leaving only a dry husk,
will I then, at the last,
be allowed to hold my treasure?

And if I do, if when his eyes are dim,
his body wasted from years of sacrifice,
turning him into an old and broken man,
will my love be undiminished?

I hope and trust that when this comes
to pass, his heart will still be praising
God, his lips be singing hymns
of joy and gratitude;

but, if the doubts of age
threaten to invade the fortress
of his confidence, and doubts assail
as darkness deepens, will my faith,
growing fainter, yet untarnished
and nurtured here in loneliness and prayer,
light his failing eyes and guide his faltering steps
on the long journey home?

Godgifu

Lady Godiva of Coventry: 1010-1067

She challenged the poverty and injustice of the age,
and when tears and arguments failed to hold much sway,
instead of reacting to bureaucracy with righteous rage,
she chose radical non-violent action to win the day.
The hair she'd brushed a hundred times each night
shone and shimmered, falling like a gown
to cover her nakedness and hide from curious sight
the beauty of her body as she rode through town.
To protect her modesty the people all agreed
to close their shutters and look the other way
until she'd passed, so that there'd be no need
to witness her sacrificial act that day –
except for a boy whose cheating left this legacy behind:
for watching Godiva riding by, Peeping Tom went blind.

Hildegard: doctor of the Church
Hildegard of Bingen: 1098-1179

Hildegard believed that herbs for the body's healing
had a part to play, with prayer, in the soul's salvation;
and perceiving the greening of earth and heaven
from far beyond our human understanding,
she celebrated Viriditas, the force that flows
through all that's green and good, in all that grows.

Like many other women since,
she posed a challenge to the Church,
displaying a deep learning never found
in books the clergy knew,
communicated in an alphabet they couldn't read,
and if they could, they wouldn't understand.

Down the centuries we hear her songs of glory
soaring higher in ripieno praise,
above the black-clad choir stalls
and dusty academic libraries
of those who failed to grasp that wisdom
could be grounded in a woman's native wit.

As she joins the other doctors of the Church:
Térèse, Theresa, Catherine of Sienna,
along with sundry men, the question hovers:
will those without a voice today
nine hundred years from now be heard,
admired?

Edward mourns for Eleanor

Eleanor of Castile: 1241-1290
'whom living we dearly cherished, and whom dead
*we cannot cease to love' ***

Despite her tender years, she was my chosen bride,
although you never welcomed her. She bore me offspring
and gave you a royal heir, but was painfully aware
of your rejection and dislike. It's rare for a marriage
of convenience to bring such happiness and love,
but she and I were blessed in our relationship.
She joined me on the Eighth Crusade and so was there
to tend my wounds; she made my house and garden
beautiful, enriched not only me but the whole nation
with her love of poetry and song. By night she lay
within my arms, by day she entertained me as we shared
talk and laughter. Would she laugh now to see my tears
and the dozen crosses I've had fashioned out of stone
to trace the route her body took on her last journey home?

* from a letter King Edward I wrote to the Abbot of Cluny in 1291, requesting
his prayers for Eleanor's soul.

Transfigured

Beatrice, in The Divine Comedy: 1266-1290

When Dante met Beatrice, he believed she might
accompany him as he was transported
to paradise, purifying his human sight

to witness the heavenly vision, unsupported
by Virgil in the circles of the blest.
When he later wrote his poem, he reported

the saints' virtues and their life of perfect rest
as well as his love for Beatrice, the divine
Muse who welcomed him as an honoured guest

and journeyed with him upwards through the nine
heavens as, humbly, they approached that height
where sorrows turn to joy, water to wine.

He dreamed her face became ever more bright
as Beatrice guided him towards God's holy light.

Mother Julian & the astronauts
Julian of Norwich: 1342-1416

To land that seminal image of a tiny blue
ball spinning in the immensity of space,
modern astronauts had to study
physics, technology and mathematics
to develop a craft that could defy
the out-of-bounds beyond earth's atmosphere,
while simultaneously learning how to seal
in a mechanical light box all that the eye revealed.
More than six hundred years ago
a woman who had seen no further
than the four walls of her cell
was moved to describe this fragile sphere
as a hazel nut held in the palm of a hand,
secure and treasured there.

Itching to go
Margery Kempe of King's Lynn: 1373-1438

Go Margery, go: set your sights
on Canterbury, Rome, Jerusalem,
as you seek relief from itching body
and from tortured soul.

Scratch until the too frail skin
begins to bleed; you need to be
absolved from sin before you can
become the bride of Christ.

As you leave respectability
of home and husband, are you
chasing visions of divinity
or fleeing from them?

The body that over many years bore
fourteen children, is now borne on waves
as you set sail in pilgrim's scallop shell
over the oceans of your tears.

Though ostracised by fellow-travellers
who fear your fervour, and accused
of heresy by the Church, nothing
can dampen your desire to preach.

While you travel in search of mystical marriage,
an earthly husband waits at home for you,
fights the law on your behalf, pays all your debts,
freeing you to wander where you will.

Sic et non

Heloïse from Paris: 1101-1164

Is your name Heloïse?
  Yes, that's the name my parents
  gave me at my birth;
  but no, I gave away that name,
  along with my identity,
  when I took the veil.

Did you accept the tutor your uncle chose for you?
  Yes, I was grateful that he understood
  my restless spirit and my need for education
  to challenge and control my wayward spirit;
  but I was nervous that his choice might be
  a subtle way in which to clip my wings,
  effectively control me.

Was it necessary that you should study Greek and Latin?
  Yes, to understand the Scriptures, stimulate
  my God-given brain; but no,
  I admit that these are not the skills I use in daily life
  or texts I need to know.

Did you find the young philosopher attractive?
  No, at first I was fascinated only by his mind,
  his breadth of knowledge and scholarship
  of a kind I hadn't met before.
  Then yes, oh yes: he set my heart on fire.

Did you both concentrate on conjugations and declensions?
  Yes, we concentrated on the joys of conjugal love.
  And no, in time I did not decline his advances.

Did Abelard take advantage of your innocence?
  Yes, perhaps he was the first to read
  and then translate the stirrings

that swept us both along;
But no, strictly he did not seduce me,
rather he gave me a wide vocabulary of Greek
and Latin words and guided my first
clumsy efforts at fitting them together
to produce sound sense.
He gave me words I lacked
to describe and celebrate
the human anatomy,
and when I'd mastered those
he delved still deeper
into his store of words,
into my secret chambers.

Were lust and fornication the result of educating a young woman?
    Yes, they followed as night follows day, but
    no, if the blood had not coursed
    so fast and free through our young veins,
    it might then have been different.

Do you regret what happened, confess that you have sinned,
accept the punishment you both endured?
    Yes, I know the rules, and do admit
    I broke them; and though I can't repent
    of my love for Abelard, I do, of course, regret
    what followed after, when I lost both love
    and freedom. But no, I will not lament
    the fact that for a time he gave me
    more love and freedom than I'd ever known
    before, or will again.

Have you maintained contact with the sinner since he entered the
monastic life?
    Yes, we correspond by letter; mine
    full of pain and passion, his
    curiously cold and factual.

No, we do not truly reach each other
in this way, for neither of us find it possible
to communicate what we long to say.

*Have you found contentment in following the will of God and of the
Church?*
    Yes, day follows day according to
    a simple pattern that leaves no need
    or inclination to think;
    but no, contentment has fled away
    for ever, and will not now be found
    within the cloister.

Do you believe in the power of love?
    Yes, my love has not diminished or abated
    despite the cruel treatment my man of God received.
    But no, it seems the love we thought was strong enough
    to rend the gates of heaven and hell,
    failed to protect us and inevitably fell
    when it met the fury of the clergy.

*'Sic et non' (Yes and no), is the name of the treatise by the mediaeval
philosopher, Peter Abelard.*

More about the women and the poems

Chiara Offreduccio

Chiara Offreduccio was born in the Italian town of Assisi in 1194, into a wealthy family, and was, from childhood, devout. When, at the age of eighteen, she heard Francis preach, her life was changed. She visited Francis at the chapel of the Porziuncula, where she had her hair cut off, took to wearing a veil and on Francis's direction went to live with a Benedictine order. Her father attempted to force her to return home, but she clung to the altar and removed her veil to show her cropped head. Clare later formed the Order of Poor Ladies of San Damiano which later became known as the Poor Clares.

My poem, *Chiara*, was one of those amazing 'gift poems', arriving fully-formed so that I had to scribble it down quickly while on a journey; and it required hardly any editing afterwards. I did not know why I had suddenly written about St Clare, whom I had not thought about for thirty years. Looking back, I remembered that on a family visit to Assisi when my children were very small, I was moved to feel sorry for Clare. Those who have been to Assisi will know the story of her devotion to St Francis and the fact that when he embraced the monastic life he persuaded her to become a nun. She undertook numerous good works, and in time became the founder of the Order of Poor Clares. While in no way wishing to diminish her genuine piety and spirituality, I could not help feeling that ending up in a convent might not have been quite what she had in mind when she was attracted to Francis and left her father's house to follow him. There were, of course, advantages to the monastic life for women at this stage of history, providing the possibility of independence and an education that they would have been unlikely to enjoy otherwise. But I was also aware that Clare probably shared all the passion, enthusiasm and confusion of other teenagers — and that she loved Francis deeply. It would appear that this sympathy of mine for Clare, and divergence from the normal hagiography, had lain dormant until it suddenly and unexpectedly erupted in this poem.

Lady Godiva

How does a legend arise, and what purpose does it serve? Is myth the opposite of history, or can it elucidate the rather sparse hard facts that we inherit? And if the story of a noblewoman performing a highly unlikely action persists down through nearly a thousand years, what does that tell us of the period in which she lived and the hopes and beliefs of the intervening years? It was questions like these that aroused my interest in the Lady Godiva story, so universally known in Britain, and so variously interpreted and illustrated down the years.

Godiva is, without doubt, an historical figure. She was an Anglo-Saxon gentlewoman who lived between around 1040 and 1080 and was married to Leofric, Earl of Mercia. The correct form of her name, Godgifu, was common in Anglo-Saxon England and is the name by which she would have been known before it was Latinised into the now familiar form of Godiva. We know that Godgifu was wealthy in her own right and that she was in all probability considerably younger than her husband. We also know that the couple were both generous benefactors, and that together they founded an abbey in Coventry.

When it comes to the famous ride, it is difficult to disentangle fact from fantasy. There are no contemporary records of it, the first mention of the story occurring in a document written by two monks in St Albans nearly a century after her death. They place the ride in 1057, and relate how Godgifu pleaded with her husband to relieve the people of their onerous taxes and how he, in a fit of pique at her persistent entreaties, agreed to do so if she would ride naked through the town square. In a spirit of generosity, she conceded to the deal and rode through the town on horseback, her body hidden by nothing more than her hair.

Other aspects of the story that appear in the various accounts include Godiva's instruction to the townspeople to close their shutters and remain indoors so that no one should witness her shame, and the fact that Leofric did, indeed, revoke the taxes. A rather charming endorsement of this part of the story comes from Ranulf Higden (died 1364) in his Polychronicon, where he mentions the fact that Leofric freed the town from all tolls except those on horses. At the time of Edward I it was found that no tolls except those on horses were being paid in Coventry. Another later accretion to the story is the appearance of Peeping Tom, who disobeyed the instruction to refrain from observing Godiva's nakedness and who was punished with blindness.

The level of Godiva's sacrifice demonstrated by the story should not be underestimated. The name Godgifu means Gift of God, and a woman who performed such a self-sacrificial action for the sake of the people would most certainly have been seen as a gift from God. It is quite reasonable to suggest that in this story we have a respectable woman who makes what must have been for her the ultimate sacrifice for the good of her people. In other words, far from Godgifu being a salacious tale told for the titillation of men, it is actually a parable in which a woman is portrayed as an image of Christ.

In my sonnet, I celebrate this good and holy woman who, for the sake of the poor and downtrodden, performed a sacrificial act through which she was able to alleviate the misery of the people of Coventry.

Hildegard, OSB

Hildegard of Bingen could be described as a Renaissance Woman, long before that term was coined (for men) or the Renaissance dawned. She was a poet, musician, theologian, composer, artist, doctor, botanist, philosopher, environmentalist, singer, herbalist, preacher, lexicographer and visionary – and it would be no idle claim to call her an early feminist.

Hildegard was born in the German Rhineland and given to the Church when she was 8 years old. As an adult she became Mother Superior of her order at St Disibod, but having come into conflict with church authorities, she founded a new abbey at Rupertsberg near Bingen in 1150, taking many of her nuns with her. Although sometimes controversial and not above bitter arguments with clergy, she was enormously respected in her lifetime and, as well as preaching widely in Europe, she regularly corresponded with a number of popes.

Her beautiful, ethereal music has grown in popularity in recent years, as well as some of her mystical art, which was inspired by her visions and set out in her major prose works: *Scivias, Liber Vitae Meritorum* and *Liber Divinorum Operum*. She also practised medical and herbalist sciences, transcribed her own music and invented her own script. Her medical knowledge was extensive, and although some of her prescriptions sound strange to modern ears, she is credited with having effected many cures.

This poem was written for a book about Hildegard, published in Italy in 2012 on the occasion of Pope Benedict XVI naming Hildegard a Doctor of the Church. It also formed part of an exhibition of my poetry mounted in Winchester Cathedral when I was Poet in Residence for that city's Ten Day Arts Festival in 2013. The poems were set in appropriate places all around the cathedral, and because of its subject matter, this one was placed below the pulpit.

Eleanor of Castile
Eleanor was barely thirteen years old when she was given in marriage to the prince who later became Edward I of England. Although a marriage of convenience, the couple appear to have enjoyed a long, happy and loving relationship, but Eleanor was initially unpopular with the populace. She probably did not speak English, and she was distrusted partly because of her business acumen in acquiring lands and property.

Eleanor's first child, who did not survive, was born when Eleanor was still only thirteen, and she went on to bear as many as another fifteen children, only about half of whom made it to adulthood. Her last son, Edward of Caernarvon, was to become Edward II.

Edward was grief-stricken when Eleanor, at the age of forty-nine, died in the village of Harby near Lincoln, when they were travelling to visit some of Eleanor's properties. Eleanor's body was embalmed, and then borne in great state to London. The cortège stopped each night on the journey, and Edward subsequently gave orders for stone memorial crosses to be erected at each of the twelve places where her body had rested: Lincoln, Grantham, Stamford, Geddington, Hardingstone (near Northampton), Stony Stratford, Woburn, Dunstable, St Albans, Waltham, Westcheap and Charing. These became known as Eleanor Crosses: only three of them now survive, and even those lack the tall crosses that originally surmounted them. The well-known monument at Charing Cross station in London was, in fact, built in 1865 to publicise the railway hotel; the original Charing Cross having been at the top of Whitehall.

Beatrice Portinari

The Divine Comedy (Divina Commedia), by Dante Alighieri, was written between the years 1308 and 1320, and describes the poet's vision of a journey through the afterlife, starting in Hell, proceeding through Purgatory and finally entering Paradise. In the first two cantos Dante is guided through Hell and Purgatory by the Roman poet, Virgil who, being pre-Christ, Dante assumed could not enter Paradise. Instead, his guide and muse for the third canto is Beatrice, Dante's ideal and idealised woman, whom the poet had met briefly when they were children, and loved from a distance ever since.

I have used the poetic form, terza rima in this poem, as that is the form used by Dante in his masterpiece.

Julian of Norwich

Julian was an anchorite, a mystic, and the author of *Revelations of Divine Love*, written in about 1395, which is the first book in English known to have been written by a woman. Her anchorite's cell was built into the wall of the church of St Julian in Norwich, England, from which she took her name. This church is now a place of pilgrimage, known as the Julian shrine.

Many of Julian's images are well-known and well-loved. For instance, T S Eliot in *Little Gidding* quotes her words *'All shall be well, … and all manner of thing shall be well'*, and her vision of the world as a tiny hazel nut held in the hand of God, to which I refer in this poem, has become a classic of Christian spirituality.

The *Revelations of Divine Love* were important to me as a teenager and young adult, so I was delighted when, through a series of chance events, I got to know Robert Llewellyn, the chaplain at the Julian Shrine, and visited him on a number of occasions. I was also given opportunities to share my love of this mystic with others, both through my writing and my speaking engagements.

Margery Kempe

Margery was born in King's Lynn, formerly known as Bishop's Lynn, in North Norfolk, where her merchant father, John Brunham, was both mayor of the town and a Member of Parliament. She married John Kempe in 1394 and bore at least fourteen children. Following the birth of her first child, she was ill for many months with what may possibly have been a form of post-natal depression, during which she saw demons and had suicidal thoughts.

She then had a vision of Jesus Christ in which she participated in the first of many conversations with him, and on occasion with his mother, Mary. Her visions were extremely vivid, and included sounds and smells as well as sight. Christ assured her that her sins were forgiven, though for the rest of her life she seems to have been obsessed with her guilt, frequently weeping and wailing over some unspecified sins. Her health remained poor, and she was tortured by intensive physical itching all her life. She somehow persuaded her husband to agree to a *chaste marriage*, though she had at least one more child after reaching this agreement.

Margery visited Julian of Norwich to seek her blessing, and began to travel extensively, making pilgrimages not only to Canterbury, but much further afield to Rome, Santiago de Compostella, Bethlehem and Jerusalem, preaching and urging people to repent and live holier lives.

Heloïse d'Argenteuil

The story of the mediaeval lovers, Abelard and Heloïse, is well-known, and has formed the basis of at least one popular film.

Heloïse is generally acknowledged as a formidable scholar in her own right. When the philosopher, Peter Abelard, found he could not afford to live in his house while studying, he contacted Heloïse's uncle, Canon Fulbert, and offered to tutor the niece in return for his accommodation. The couple became lovers, and when Heloïse became pregnant, Abelard persuaded her, much against her wishes, to marry him. Fulbert's revenge was to arrange for men to forcibly castrate Abelard, following the shame of which Abelard became a monk at the abbey of St Denis, in Paris. He also managed to persuade his former lover to enter the religious life herself. Although the couple continued to correspond, Abelard claimed not to have loved her, but only to have lusted after her, and claimed that they were being punished for their sin.

Abelard's major philosophical work was 'Sic et Non' (Yes and No), which is why I have, in this poem, used the devise of a judge posing a series of questions to Heloïse, each followed by both negative and positive replies on her part.

Indigo Dreams Publishing
24 Forest Houses
Halwill
Beaworthy
Devon
EX21 5UU
www.indigodreams.co.uk